Don't miss these other record-breaking books!

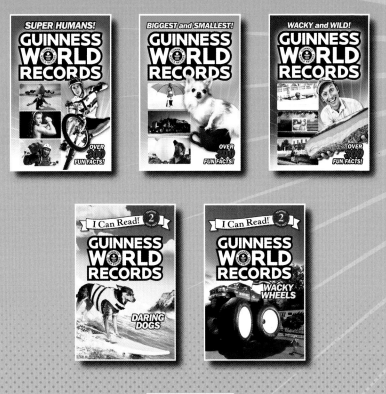

GUINNESS WORLD RECORDS

INCREDIBLE ANIMALS!

by **CHRISTA ROBERTS**

HARPER
An Imprint of HarperCollinsPublishers

Library of Congress Control Number: 2015952474
ISBN 978-0-06-234167-9

Design by Victor Joseph Ochoa
20   SCP   10 9 8 7
❖
First Edition

Guinness World Records holders are truly amazing, but all attempts
to set or break records are performed under controlled conditions
and at the participant's own risk. Please seek out the appropriate
guidance before you attempt any record-breaking activities.

TABLE OF CONTENTS

INTRODUCTION
6

CHAPTER 1: Dog-Gone Amazing
7

CHAPTER 2: Fantastic Felines
45

CHAPTER 3: Hooves, Humps, and Fleece
60

CHAPTER 4: Cute Companions and Primo Primates
80

CHAPTER 5: Rabbits! Snakes! Scales! And More . . .
89

CHAPTER 6: Feathers and Fins
102

CHAPTER 7: We Love Animals
109

INTRODUCTION

Anyone, anywhere, has the potential to be a record-breaker! For over 60 years, Guinness World Records (GWR) has timed, weighed, measured, verified, and documented thousands of the world's record-breakers in every category that you can imagine. There are over 40,000 current records!

Record-breaking is free to do. If the GWR adjudicators (the official judges who confirm records) approve your idea for a new record—or if you can prove you've bettered an existing title—you're on your way to becoming Officially Amazing!

Incredible Animals! features animals with paws, claws, feathers, wings, beaks, hooves, and scales that have defied the odds to earn a Guinness World Records title. You'll hang out with pets like Cupcake, the smallest service dog; Colo, the oldest living gorilla in captivity; Happie, the skateboarding goat; and more! This book has over 90 jaw-dropping achievements that have earned these unbelievable animals a record.

Maybe you—and an animal friend—will be inspired to go after a record or two of your own after reading these real-life stories. The next edition of this book could include a new world record holder: **YOU!**

A dog can be your best friend, and it's easy to see why. Our pooches protect us, keep us company, and love us no matter what. The four-legged friends you'll meet in these pages are a paw above the rest. In this chapter, you'll be introduced to a pack of real-life canine wonders, including the world's tallest dog ever, the smallest service dog, and dogs that skateboard, skip, and surf!

SAY "AHHHHH!"

Augie, a golden retriever owned by the Miller family in Dallas, Texas, started down the road to fame when he was five years old. He won a national contest that earned him $5,000, a trip to New York City, and tickets to see a live David Letterman show! Although he didn't appear on *Letterman*, he was a contestant on Animal Planet's *Pet Star*. And three years later, he officially became a Guinness World Records holder. His special trick? Augie holds the record for the **most tennis balls held in the mouth by a dog**. This retriever can open his mouth wide enough to fit five tennis balls! And he did just that on July 6, 2003. Advantage, Augie!

A RECORD-SETTING LEAP

Cinderella May is a Holly Grey—a type of greyhound—owned by Kate Long and Kathleen Conroy of Miami, Florida. Known for their strong bodies and speed, greyhounds love to run and play and compete in agility competitions and races. At the Purina Pro Plan Incredible Dog Challenge National Finals in Missouri, Cinderella May was the belle of the ball. She wowed the crowd and cleared a lofty 68 inches—the **highest jump by a dog**. Now that's something to wag your tail over!

"EARS" LOOKING AT YOU!

If you ask **Harbor** if his ears hang low, the answer would be a definite "woof!" Harbor, a black-and-tan coonhound, had his ears measured at 12.25 inches (left ear) and 13.5 inches (right ear) on June 8, 2010, making him the Guinness World Records holder for the **longest ears on a living dog**. His owner, Jennifer Wert of Colorado, says that when he was a puppy, Harbor frequently tripped on his long ears. "It's really fun to be the owner of a Guinness World Records holder," Jennifer says. "Cars will literally stop in the street to take a closer look and get a picture!"

ULTIMATE FACT:

Harbor's long ears actually help him smell—not hear—better. When moving around, his ears will fall into a rhythm that helps sweep scents into his nose.

LISTEN UP

The dog with the **longest ears ever** is **Tigger**, a bloodhound who was owned by Bryan and Christina Flessner of St. Joseph, Illinois. His ears measured 13.75 inches (right ear) and 13.5 inches (left ear). Sadly, Tigger passed away in 2009, but during his lifetime, he won many show titles and over 180 best of breed awards. Tigger was inducted into the Bloodhound Hall of Fame in 2003.

THE GREENEST DOG IN THE WORLD

If you thought a dog couldn't be eco-friendly, think again. A Labrador named **Tubby**, owned by Sandra Gilmore of Pontnewydd, Wales, UK, has helped recycle a whopping 26,000 plastic bottles over a period of six years, the **most bottles recycled by a dog**. He collects the discarded bottles on his daily walks, crushes them, and then passes them to Sandra. "He'll dig them out from anywhere and go under bushes and even into water to fetch them," Sandra says. When the local town council heard about it, they gave Tubby a reward that any dog would love: a juicy bone!

TONGUE WAGGIN' TITLES

Having a long tongue sure comes in handy if you're a dog—think of how much water these four-legged friends could lap up! The current **longest tongue on a dog** belongs to **Puggy**, a male Pekingese owned by Becky Stanford. Puggy's tongue was measured at 4.5 inches at the Avondale Haslet Animal Clinic in Texas on May 8, 2009, when Puggy was nine years old. Puggy is 13 inches tall—that means his tongue is one third the height of his entire body!

TOTALLY LICKED

The **longest tongue on a dog ever** belonged to **Brandy**, a boxer who lived with her owner, John Scheid, in Michigan. Brandy's tongue grew to an incredible 17 inches long—so long, it couldn't even fit inside her mouth!

HANG TEN

If you were at Ocean Beach Dog Beach in San Diego, California, on October 18, 2011, you might have looked out at the water and thought you were seeing things. That was the day that **Abbie Girl**, an Australian kelpie, achieved a world record, beating out more than 20 other *paw*-ticipants by surfing a 351.7-foot wave—the **longest wave surfed by a dog**.

Kelpies are an Australian dog breed used to herd sheep by jumping on their backs to steer them. No doubt Abbie Girl's natural balance helped her stay on the surfboard.

Abbie Girl's owner, Michael Uy, discovered she could surf by chance when she followed him into the water and he put her on his surfboard to rest. Instead, she stood up and rode a wave all the way in. And that's how a shy rescue dog became a record-setting surfer!

PARTY POPPER

Cally the Wonderdog, a Jack Russell, really knows how to go out with a bang! She and her owner, Mitch Jenkins, from the UK, achieved the **fastest time to pop 100 balloons by a dog**—41.67 seconds—on the set of *Britain's Got Talent Live* on May 25, 2015. The following month they paid a visit to Guinness World Records HQ in London, UK, to give a noisy demonstration and receive their certification (below).

BALANCING ACT

Walking on a tightrope requires focus and balance, something that **Ozzy**, a border collie–Australian kelpie cross, has in spades. He achieved the record for **fastest crossing of a tightrope** in 18.22 seconds at the F.A.I.T.H. Animal Rescue in Norfolk, UK. Ozzy lives with his owner, Nick Johnson, who has no formal dog-training experience. He learned tightrope-walking techniques from the internet and trained Ozzy to cover a length of 11 feet, 5.7 inches to break the record! Border collies and kelpies are known for their agility and intensity.

ON THE NOSE

Talk about willpower! This dog really takes the cake . . . or, *ahem*, treats. **Monkey** displayed her steady sense of balance, along with her incredible patience, on the set of the TV show *Guinness World Records Unleashed* in Los Angeles, California. On July 2, 2013, Monkey was able to balance 26 treats on her nose at one time with the help of her handler, Meghan Fraser, earning her a spot in the record books for **most treats balanced on the nose**.

QUICK ON HIS PAWS

One record wasn't enough for this adorable Pomeranian. **Jiff** earned two in 2013 at TOPS Kennels in Grayslake, Illinois: the **fastest time to complete 10 meters on hind legs** and the **fastest time to complete 5 meters on front legs**. Just how speedy was he? Well, Jiff covered 32 feet, 9.6 inches on his hind legs in 6.56 seconds. Then he covered 16 feet, 4.8 inches on his front legs in 7.76 seconds. And not only is Jiff a world record holder—this pooch has some serious star power. You may have seen him showing off his astonishing moves in Katy Perry's "Dark Horse" music video!

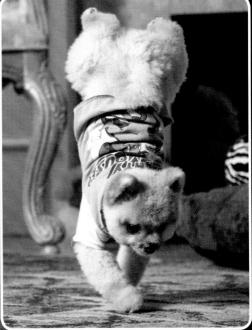

ALL TOGETHER NOW

Jumping rope isn't just for kids . . . sometimes our four-legged friends want to get in on the action! That's what happened on October 27, 2009, on the set of *Bikkuri Chojin Special #3* in Tochigi, Japan. **Uchida Geinousha's Super Wan Wan Circus** achieved the feat of having 13 dogs all skipping on the same rope, leaping straight into history as the **most dogs skipping on the same rope**. And then, on the set of *Officially Amazing* on January 17, 2013, the Super Wan Wan Circus broke their own record—this time 14 dogs all skipped on the same rope! The dogs skipped 16 times. Seven of the 14 dogs were first-time record challengers, but the other seven were old pros, having taken part in the previous record attempt. Truly an incredible sight!

DOUBLE DUTCH DYNAMO

Hop, skip, and a jump! **Geronimo**, a female border collie–kelpie cross who was adopted from a facility in Missouri, is one dog who's quick on her paws. This remarkable pooch loves to skip, and her passion has morphed from a hobby into making her a multiple world record holder. Geronimo holds the record for the **most double Dutch–style skips in one minute**—128—achieved on the set of NBC's *Today* on April 7, 2014, in New York City. She also holds the record for the **most jump-rope skips in one minute**. How many did she do? A whopping 91! Geronimo also has a knack for agility and Frisbee tricks.

DISC DOG

Teaching a dog to catch one Frisbee can be a bit of a challenge. Not so for American Edward Watson, it seems. His dog, **Rose**, didn't simply master catching one—she can catch *seven* Frisbees, thrown one at a time, and hold them all in her mouth at once! No surprise that she set the record for the **most flying discs caught in the mouth**.

SCOOT OVER!

In **Norman**'s neighborhood, it's not just kids who ride scooters—dogs do, too! Or rather, *dog*. Once this Briard got his paws on a scooter, he was hooked. Norman's 98-foot ride at the All-Tournament Players Park in Georgia on July 12, 2013, was achieved in 20.77 seconds, earning him both his world record for the **fastest 30 meters on a scooter**—*and* his nickname, Norman the Scooter Dog. Norman's owner and trainer, Karen Cobb, says she always knew that Norman was special. "He picked things up really quickly," she says.

How did he ride his way into the record books? Well, Norman begins by balancing himself on the scooter with his two front paws on the handle. With one back paw on the scooter, he uses his other to push off.

And if being a scooter pro wasn't already amazing enough, he's also able to ride a bike with training wheels, earning him the record for the **fastest 30 meters on a bicycle by a dog**. Get out of the way for Norman.

TINY HELPER

Size definitely doesn't matter when it comes to helping others. And the proof is in the pudding . . . or rather, **Cupcake**. This vegetable-loving, long-haired, pint-sized Chihuahua is the world's **smallest service dog**, measuring 6.25 inches tall. Her owner, Angela Bain of New Jersey, says that when she saw Cupcake, she knew this special dog was the one for her. "It was the greatest day in my whole life," Angela says of the day she brought Cupcake home.

FRIEND TO THE END

Donna was a hearing guide dog owned by John Hogan of New South Wales, Australia. Before she died on May 6, 1995, at the age of 20 years, 2 months, Donna had completed eight years of active service in New Zealand and ten years in Australia helping people who were deaf or hard of hearing. That work and dedication makes Donna the **longest-serving hearing dog**. By alerting her human companions to important sounds, such as doorbells, telephones, or alarms, Donna provided an invaluable service to those she helped.

A CANINE FORCE TO BE RECKONED WITH

Being small doesn't mean you can't be tough. And no one knows that better than Sheriff Dan McClelland, owner of **Midge**, the world's **smallest police dog**. Midge, a Chihuahua–rat terrier cross who measures 11 inches tall and 23 inches long, works as an official law enforcement work dog—also known as a police K9—at the Geauga County Sheriff's Office in Chardon, Ohio.

Once Midge passed her Ohio certification as a narcotics dog on November 7, 2006, it meant that her actions are recognized by the courts, and she can be used for arrests, search warrants, and more. Midge doesn't need to sit and wait at the station—she gets to be a part of the action! The Chihuahua accompanies Sheriff McClelland on all his meetings and call responses. Midge is small enough to search school lockers (completing her first at only six months old)!

IN THE DOGHOUSE

Even dogs can do time. A Lhasa apso named **Word** holds the record for the **longest time on doggy death row**. He waited eight years and 190 days for his fate to be determined. Word was initially incarcerated at the Seattle Animal Shelter on May 4, 1993, following two biting incidents. After living most of his life in confinement, Word was released on November 10, 2001, when he was transported to the Pigs Peace Sanctuary in Washington and lived out the rest of his days there.

SHORT HAIR, LONG LEGS

The world's **tallest dog ever** would have towered over most kindergartners! **Zeus**, a Great Dane owned by Denise Doorlag and her family in Michigan, measured 3 feet, 8 inches on October 4, 2011. Sadly, Zeus passed away in September 2014, and the search is now on to find the current **tallest male dog**.

TALL GIRL

The **tallest female dog living** is **Lizzy**, who measured 3 feet, 1.96 inches tall in Fort Myers, Florida, USA, on November 14, 2014.

GENTLE GIANTS

Loyal, protective, and heroic, these dogs are wonderful family pets. But you might want to think twice about letting them sleep in your bed! That's because this is one of the largest breeds on the planet. Regularly weighing between 170 and 200 pounds, adult male **Old English mastiffs** (pictured) share the Guinness World Records title for **heaviest dog breed** with the **Saint Bernard**, which can reach similar weights. They're especially suited to sub-urban environments due to their large size and exercise needs. The British Kennel Club describes the ideal mastiff as having "a large, powerful, well-knit frame" that displays "a combination of grandeur and courage."

SAVING HIS PENNIES

The next time you're thinking about spending money, remember the actions of this thrifty four-legged friend. **Pepper**, a dog owned by Claudia Neumann of Germany, knows the value of saving a penny. He holds the record for the **most coins deposited into a piggy bank in one minute**. How many coins did Pepper deposit? Seven!

NOTEWORTHY TRICK

While Pepper's a saver, **Ben**, a cross between a shih tzu and a Japanese spaniel, likes to flash his cash! This pup holds the record for the **most bank notes removed from a wallet by a dog in one minute**, taking out six during a live broadcast on German TV.

SWEET VICTORIES

Sweet Pea is not only fast—she has amazing balance! This Australian shepherd–border collie mix holds the record for the **fastest 100 meters** (328 feet) **with a soda can balanced on the head**. Her amazing time? Two minutes, 55 seconds. No word on whether anyone drank the soda after that speedy sprint! But that's not her only record-setting achievement. The **most steps walked down facing forward balancing a glass of water**—10—and the **most steps walked up facing forward balancing a glass of water**—17—are also part of her repertoire.

DOGGIE PADDLE

If you ever find yourself in trouble when you're out on the water, you'll wish this brave dog was nearby. That's because **Jack the Black**, a full-blooded Newfoundland, achieved the **fastest time to retrieve a person from the water**. Newfoundlands are known for their swimming aptitude and their lifesaving instincts, and Jack is a stellar example of his breed. On June 22, 2013, he showed off his record-setting time of 1 minute, 36.812 seconds on the Kaarster See, a lake in Germany, by pulling a mock victim a distance of 82 feet to shore. Jack is a completely trained and certified search-and-rescue dog, and works with his handler, Hans-Joachim Brueckmann, for the German rescue organization DLRG.

STOKED TO SKATE

One of the coolest skateboard dudes around happens to have four paws instead of two feet. And these paws know how to travel. On July 30, 2009, **Tillman** the English bulldog covered a 328-foot stretch in 19.678 seconds during X Games 15 in California—the **fastest 100 meters** (328 feet) **on a skateboard**. Tillman loves being active and lives the California dream—he can also surf, snowboard, and skimboard! Tillman has since been overtaken by a dog named **Jumpy**, who traveled the same distance on a skateboard in 19.65 seconds while on the set of *Officially Amazing* in Los Angeles, California, on September 16, 2013.

GIRLS vs. BOYS

Can you imagine having 16 squirming, adorable puppies? Now imagine that they are *all* the same sex. That's exactly what happened when **Llana**, a greyhound-saluki mix owned by Nigel Wood, gave birth. This proud canine was the mom to the **largest litter of female puppies**, born on June 27, 1998. And a litter of same-sex boys wasn't far off: on November 29, 2004, **Tia**, a Neapolitan mastiff owned by Damian Ward and Anne Kellegher in the UK, gave birth to the **largest litter of male puppies**: 15!

LIVING SMALL

Chihuahuas are known for being little, but **Milly** takes it to a whole new level: 3.8 inches to be exact! She's the **shortest dog** in the world—small enough to fit in the palm of your hand or in your shoe! Milly was born on December 1, 2011, and is owned by Vanesa Semler of Dorado, Puerto Rico.

CANINE COVER GIRL

Whoever said dogs can't work it for the camera hasn't met **Bebe**, the **smallest modeling dog**. This four-year-old long-haired Chihuahua, who measures 6.75 inches tall and 9.5 inches long, has strutted her stuff for websites, publications, and television appearances—and was paid to do it! She's owned by Nikki Figular from New Jersey.

WHAT A WOOF!

Everyone in this golden retriever's neighborhood knows who **Charlie** is—he's the dog with the **loudest bark**! It measured 113.1 decibels (dB) during the Purina Bark in the Park event held in Adelaide, Australia, on October 20, 2012.

WHO LET THE DOGS BARK?

If folks living near Washington Park, Colorado, were trying to sleep in on November 7, 2009, they were out of luck. That's because it was on that day that the **loudest bark by a group of dogs** was measured at 124 dB in an event organized by **Petmate**. All the ruckus was for a good cause: pet owners were asked to donate cans of dog food for local dog rescue centers. We'll bark to that!

SAVING LIVES

In 2003, **Armstrong**, a yellow Labrador retriever in California, became the **first diabetes-detection dog**. He was trained to use his powerful sense of smell to detect the chemical changes that happen in a person's body that can cause hypoglycemia—low blood sugar. This is extremely important because if this condition isn't caught, a person with diabetes can potentially die. Armstrong was so good at detecting diabetes that Dogs for Diabetics, a charity that trains diabetes-detection dogs, was founded in 2004.

HOME, SUITE, HOME

Getting sent to the doghouse wouldn't be so bad if you're one of the privileged and pampered Great Danes who call Barkingham Palace home. The world's **most expensive pet home** was designed by acclaimed architect **Andy Ramus** at a cost of more than $380,000. Located in Gloucestershire, UK, it includes retinal scanners, climate control, private playgrounds, a state-of-the-art stereo system, TVs, automatic food and water dispensers, and of course, a treats cupboard!

BOWWOW VOW

Everyone knows weddings can be expensive. But this one really takes the dog biscuit! **Baby Hope Diamond**, a Coton de Tulear, and **Chilly Pasternak**, a Virginia poodle, exchanged their "vows" at the Jurimuah Essex Hotel in New York City on July 12, 2012. The wedding was estimated to cost over $270,000, making it the **most expensive pet wedding**! Most of the wedding elements were donated in order to raise money and awareness for the Humane Society of New York.

CHAPTER 2
Fantastic Felines

F rom curious kittens to purring cats, fluffy Persians to brown tabbies, we just can't get enough of these popular pets. They make us laugh as they stalk imaginary prey, pounce on toys, and explore their surroundings. The felines in this chapter have extraordinary abilities. You'll meet a cat that's shorter than a pencil, the oldest cat ever, and a cat who once called the White House home, along with some others that are definitely the cat's meow!

STEWIE FOR SHORT

Stewie, the world's **longest domestic cat ever**, beat the competition paws down. The Maine coon, whose full name was Mymains Stewart Gilligan, measured an incredible 4 feet, 0.5 inches when he was fully stretched out. After countless people commented on his length, his owner, Robin Hendrickson from Nevada, decided to see if he was record-worthy, and the rest is history. Stewie, who passed away in 2013, was a certified therapy animal, and Robin said that Stewie loved meeting new people.

STANDING TALL

She might be shorter than a bottle of water, but this feline stands head and shoulders above the competition. **Lilieput**, a nine-year-old female munchkin, measures a mere 5.25 inches from the floor to her shoulders, making her the **shortest living cat**. Her owner, a professional pet-sitter named Christel Young of California, found her while out walking a client's dog. Christel says she couldn't have imagined leaving the abandoned cat to fend for herself—her small stature made her extravulnerable to other animals that might harm her. Now Lilieput's short legs have walked straight into world-record history!

A PURR-*FECT JUMP!*

Cats are notorious for jumping. Sometimes they land on their feet, while other times their tumbles end up on a silly cat video. Samantha Martin's cat, **Alley**, falls into the first category by leaps and bounds. Alley is famous for jumping farther than any other domestic feline. She set the record for the **longest jump by a cat**—6 feet—on October 27, 2013, in Austin, Texas. Let's hope Alley looks before she leaps!

A HERCULEAN FEAT

If you cross a lion with a tiger, you get a liger. And at 922 pounds and standing over 4 feet at the shoulder, a liger fittingly named **Hercules** lives up to his name as the world's **largest living cat**. This adult male cat lives at Myrtle Beach Safari, a wildlife reserve in South Carolina. He shares his home with his brother Sinbad, who although taller than Hercules, is slightly lighter. Ligers are usually larger than their two parents and weigh about a hundred times more than an average house cat. If you're hoping to find a liger in the wild, it's not likely to happen, because the habitats of lions and tigers don't overlap.

NOW THAT'S TALL!

No one had any trouble spotting Savannah Islands Trouble. Known simply as **Trouble**, he was the **tallest cat ever**, measuring a full 19 inches from shoulder to the tip of his toe and weighing 20 pounds. His owner, a California cat breeder named Debby Maraspini, said she knew Trouble was going to be large, but didn't expect him to be *quite* so big. He was part domestic cat, part serval—a recognized hybrid called a Savannah, which the International Cat Association accepted as a new registered breed in 2001. Sadly, Trouble passed away in August 2012.

BY A HAIR

At Jami Smith's home in Oceanside, California, it's a good idea to keep a lint brush in every room. That's because her cat, **Sophie Smith**, boasts the **longest fur on a cat**. Sophie's fur measured in at a lengthy 10.11 inches on November 9, 2013.

GOLDEN OLDIE

If cats have nine lives, **Crème Puff** definitely lived hers to the fullest. Born on August 3, 1967, Crème Puff lived with her owner, Jake Perry, in Texas, until August 6, 2005: a whopping 38 years and 3 days, making her the **oldest cat ever**! Something was definitely in the water at the Perry household—Mr. Perry was also the owner of Grandpa Rex Allen, a former holder of the same record!

SENIOR CAT

The **oldest living cat** is **Corduroy**. Born in 1989, he was aged 25 years, 339 days, as of July 6, 2015. The mature moggy lives with his owner, Ashley Reed Okura, in Sisters, Oregon.

FIRST FELINE

One of the most popular pets to ever call the White House home was **Socks**, a stray cat rescued by a neighbor of Bill and Hillary Clinton when they lived in the governor's mansion in Little Rock, Arkansas. The future First Family adopted the stray, who would go on to be the **most popular political cat**. In 1991, when Bill Clinton became president, Socks moved into the White House and became First Cat. During his eight years "in office," Socks is said to have received 75,000 letters and packages a week! Unfortunately, Socks didn't get along with Buddy, the Labrador retriever who joined the Clintons in 1997. So when President Clinton's time in office was over, they left Socks in the care of his secretary, Betty Currie.

RICH KITTY

Everyone knew how much Ben Rea of the UK loved his cats. And when he died in May 1988, he definitely left his cat **Blackie** a little something to remember him by . . . $12.5 million! That's right, the millionaire antiques dealer was a recluse who chose not to leave anything to his human family members. He left his entire fortune to the last surviving of his 15 cats, as well as to three different cat charities—with the stipulation that they look after his beloved pet. This made Blackie the **wealthiest cat** in the world.

PURR-*KIEST*

Merlin the cat didn't need to use any magic to earn his Guinness World Records title: he just had to think happy thoughts. When this kitty is in a good mood, he isn't shy about letting everyone know. His purr—which measured 67.8 dB on April 2, 2015—is louder than an air conditioner, earning him the record for **loudest purr by a domestic cat**. Owner Tracy Westwood from Torquay, UK, said, "Occasionally when he's really loud I have to repeat myself. Sometimes if the telephone rings I do get people asking me what's that noise in the background; I tell them it's the cat, but I don't know if they believe me."

KITTY COLLECTOR

Carmen de Aldana of Guatemala has the **largest collection of cat-related items**: 21,321! Carmen started her cat collection after buying three little ceramic kittens in 1954 when she was 13 years old (only one of the kittens still exists). She now has a private museum of cat items at her family house in Puerto Barrios, Guatemala. Of the 23,007 pieces in her collection, 21,321 items are counted because they are not duplicates.

THE GREATEST MOUSER

Catching mice comes naturally to cats, but one prolific mouser took her responsibility very seriously. **Towser** was a female tortoiseshell owned by Glenturret Distillery in Scotland. Mice are attracted to barley in the distillery, and so Glenturret used Towser to keep the rodent population under control. And she more than lived up to the task. Towser is estimated to have caught a whopping three mice per day, adding up to an estimated 29,000 mice, making her the **greatest mouser**! No doubt about it: Towser's mouse-catching skills were the cat's pajamas. The city she lived in agreed: they erected a statue in her honor.

BY A WHISKER . . .

Do you know what helps a cat figure out how wide an opening is—and if it will fit through it? Whiskers! These ultrasensitive feline mood indicators are vital to a cat's sensory function. **Missi**, a Maine coon, holds the record for the **longest cat whiskers**. Hers measure 7.5 inches. A cat's whiskers should never, ever be trimmed. Not only isn't it necessary, it can cause a cat to become extremely disoriented, making it difficult for them to walk, run, and judge distances correctly.

BEAUTIFUL MEOW-SIC

Catcerto, composed by **Mindaugas Piečaitis** of Lithuania, is a four-minute piano concerto for chamber orchestra and cat. The piece, in which the orchestra accompanies a video recording of a cat pawing at keys on a piano, is the **first piano concerto for a cat**. It debuted at the Klaipèda Concert Hall in Lithuania on June 5, 2009, with Nora the cat at the piano. Composer-conductor Piečaitis notated Nora's melody from a video recording he had seen on YouTube, then composed the orchestral accompaniment to match. The piece requires the orchestra to play live alongside Nora's projected video footage. Nora is a rescue cat from Cherry Hill, New Jersey, and was named Cat of the Year in the annual ASPCA Humane Awards.

If you never thought a pig or a camel could be a world record holder, think again. Get to know the world's tallest horse. Be inspired by a little pony who has cheered up countless children. And see that pigs really *can* fly (almost)!

WHAT A PORKER!

The **largest pig ever** recorded was a Poland China hog named **Big Bill**. This pig was quite an oinker: he measured 5 feet to the shoulder and 9 feet long in 1933. At the time of his death, he weighed 2,552 pounds and was on his way to appear in an exhibition at the Chicago World's Fair.

A HAPPY BIRTH-DAY

The **most calves in a single birth** is five, all of which were born to **Coneja Roja** ("Red Rabbit") on March 18, 2005, at the Santa Clara Ranch in Mexico. Coneja Roja's owners are Mr. Guadalupe Olivares Garza & Sons. It was the first pregnancy for Coneja Roja, and each of her calves weighed 35 pounds. All of them currently live at the Santa Clara Ranch.

HIGH HORSE

There are big horses—and then there's **Big Jake**, a Belgian gelding who lives in Wisconsin. As of 2010, he was the **tallest living horse**, measuring 6 feet, 10.75 inches, without shoes.

LITTLE BULL

The **shortest bull** is **Chegs HH AR Golden Boy**, owned by Hearts & Hands Animal Rescue in Ramona, California. He measures a mere 2 feet, 4.2 inches from the hoof to the shoulders!

ULTIMATE FACT:

Pigs are highly trainable. Rolling a ball, dancing, understanding full sentences—all these things and more are possible for a pig!

A "PIG" LEAP

Pigs might not be able to fly, but **Kotetsu**, a potbellied pig who lives in Japan, has proven they sure can jump. He holds the record for the **highest jump by a pig**, leaping 2 feet, 3.5 inches on a farm in Japan. Kotetsu was only 18 months old when he achieved his oinkerrific record!

NAME CHANGER

The **tallest horse ever** was a shire gelding named **Sampson**, born in 1846 and bred by Thomas Cleaver of Toddington Mills, Bedfordshire, UK. Sampson was later renamed Mammoth, and his new name was on the money: he measured 7 feet, 2.5 inches in 1850 and is said to have weighed 3,359 pounds!

PONY TALE

Golden Shante, also known as Topper, has a tail that just wouldn't stop growing! At 13 feet, 5 inches, it's the **longest tail on a pony**. Topper is owned by Janine Sparks, and his tail was measured in Indiana on July 24, 2010.

MARCHING PROUD

Anyone who was in Khui Doloon Khudag in Mongolia on August 9, 2013, saw a parade unlike any other. On that day, the world's **largest horse parade** took place. A whopping 11,125 horses and their riders took part in an event organized by the **Federation of Mongolian Horse Racing Sport and Trainers** (FMHRST). The parade covered 2.49 miles and participants came from each of the 21 provinces of Mongolia. The youngest horseman was two-year-old Uurtsaih Gerelt-Od and the oldest was 90-year-old Dashchoimbal Gungaadash!

HORSE SENSE!

The **most numbers correctly identified by a horse in one minute** is 19 and was achieved by **Lukas**. He was assisted by his owner and trainer, Karen Murdock, in Walnut, California, on June 16, 2010.

MAKING A SPLASH

Everyone knows that diving into a pool on a summer day is the best way to stay cool. So is it any surprise that a pig—one of the smartest animals around—wanted to get in on the water action? When **Miss Piggy**, a pig owned by Tom Vandeleur of Australia, leaped a distance of 10 feet, 10 inches into a 34-inch-deep pool, she jumped into the record books, too, for achieving the **longest dive by a pig**.

FUR PIG

A pig dressed in sheep's clothing? It's not just a story: the **Mangalitsa pig** of Hungary is the world's **hairiest domestic pig**. Unlike all other pigs, the Mangalitsa grows a remarkably long and hairy coat that looks like the fleece of a sheep! There are three breeds, which come in different colors: the blond Mangalitsa (white), the swallow-bellied Mangalitsa (black body with white feet and belly), and the red Mangalitsa (copper).

"SOW" OLD

The **oldest pig ever** is named **Ernestine**. She was born on July 19, 1991, and lived to the ripe old age of 23 years, 76 days, before sadly passing away in October 2014. Ernestine lived with her owners, Jude and Dan King, in Calgary, Alberta, Canada.

DINKY DONKEY

Little **KneeHi**, born October 2, 2007, holds the record for the **shortest donkey**. He stands a mere 2 feet, 1.29 inches from hoof to the top of the withers (the ridge between shoulder blades). He's a registered miniature Mediterranean donkey, and is owned by James, Frankie, and Ryan Lee of Gainesville, Florida. Mediterranean donkeys were bred in Sardinia and were to be kept indoors and used to turn grinding stones to make flour.

ULTIMATE FACT: The breed was first introduced in the USA in 1929 by Robert Green, who said, "Miniature donkeys possess the affectionate nature of a Newfoundland, the resignation of a cow, the durability of a mule, the courage of a tiger, and the intellectual capability only slightly inferior to man's."

SMALL BUT MIGHTY

Thumbelina, Kay and Paul Goessling's dwarf miniature pony, might be small in stature, but that doesn't stop her from contributing to the world in a big way. She stands just 17.5 inches at the shoulder, making her the **smallest living horse**. This little brown mare, who lives on Goose Creek Farm in Missouri with her owners, works as a therapy horse and has given inspiration to countless sick and disabled children. She is pictured here meeting Radar, who previously was her record-holding opposite.

71

CHARLY HORSE

Charly, a miniature Aragon Arabian horse, who stands 25 inches at the shoulder, is the **shortest male horse**. He was born in 2007 on a minihorse farm in Holland. At the age of one and a half, Charly left his Dutch homeland and moved to Italy, where he now lives as a pet with his owner Bartolomeo Messina. Even though he's small, Charly has a BIG appetite and eats three times a day. Charly loves carrots, corn, and oats, plus carob beans, which are an important part of his diet. If he could, he'd eat all day long.

HOWDY, THERE!

Everything is big in Texas—even the donkeys! That's where **Romulus**, an American mammoth jackstock, lives with his owners Cara and Phil Yellott of Red Oak. The world's **tallest donkey** stands 5 feet, 8 inches at the shoulder, and what's even more incredible is that his brother, Remus, stands at an equally lofty 5 feet, 4 inches.

OFF TO THE RACES

With a name like **Lamborghini**, it's no surprise that this is a sheep that likes to move. He's the Guinness World Records holder for the **most races won by a sheep**, taking the number-one spot in 165 out of 179 total season races at Odds Farm Park in the UK. Not too *baaaaaaaaaaaaa*d. . . . Sounds like the odds were definitely in Lamborghini's favor!

GOAT ON WHEELS

Skateboarding is pretty common on the streets of Fort Myers, Florida. But when it's a goat on the board? Now that's gnarly! **Happie**, a Nigerian dwarf cross, traveled 118 feet on her skateboard on March 4, 2012—the **farthest distance skateboarded by a goat**. She covered that distance in only 25 seconds. She would have gone even farther except for one small problem: she hit a parking barrier!

Happie lives with Melody Cooke and her family, and they describe Happie as a much-loved family pet. When she's not skateboarding, she enjoys walking in the grass, nibbling on plants, and hanging out with her chicken and duck friends. Melody explains, "It feels like a dream. First of all she has a Guinness World Records title, second of all she skateboards—and she's a goat!"

JUST ONE OF THE TEAM

The Los Angeles County Sherriff's Department got a new member on April 5, 2003: one with a hump! That was the day **Bert**, the **highest-ranking law-enforcement camel**, was made a reserve deputy sheriff.

Bert (which stands for Be Enthusiastic, Responsible, and True) is a dromedary, which means he has one hump. He enjoys going on patrol with his handler, Reserve Deputy Nance Fite. Together they visit schools to talk to students about right and wrong. On one such visit, Bert got a kiss—from the principal! The principal had lost a bet with the students, and as a result she had to smooch the camel. Bert didn't mind!

Weighing 1,770 pounds on May 4, 2003, it's safe to say that Bert is the heaviest and hairiest reserve deputy in Los Angeles (and also has the longest eyelashes of them all!).

HORNS OF PLENTY

Lurch, an African-Watusi steer owned by Janice Wolf of Arkansas, had serious horns. So serious that their circumference measured 3 feet, 1.5 inches, the **largest horn circumference for a steer ever**. The horns were so large that two vets measured three times to confirm their incredible size. Lurch died in 2010, but his spirit lives on—a local taxidermist having made a full-size model of Lurch.

HOLY COW

Owned by Patricia Meads-Hanson, **Blosom** was the **tallest cow ever**. She measured 6 feet, 6.4 inches from the hoof to the withers in Orangeville, Illinois, on May 24, 2014. Sadly, she passed away in May 2015.

GOAT COAT

The **most expensive goat** in the world was an **Angora buck** bred in New Zealand. Why so pricey? Its beautiful and valuable fleece (mohair). The goat was sold in January 1985 to Elliot Brow Ltd. of Waipu, New Zealand, for the equivalent of $82,600!

Hamsters, gerbils, and guinea pigs are not only sky high in the adorable category, but they're some of the most playful and entertaining creatures on the planet. But make no mistake—behind the round fuzzy bodies, furry faces, and tiny quivering noses stand real superstars. Speaking of superstars, you'll also be introduced to a beloved celebrity gorilla and one of the brainiest chimps in town. Say hello to some little guys (and a few *much* larger animals!) with some very big accomplishments!

SPEED EATER

Try to guess what the **fastest-eating mammal** is. If you guessed the **star-nosed mole**, you'd be right! Research done at Vanderbilt University in Tennessee recorded an average handling time of 230 milliseconds. The fastest time? 120 milliseconds. You don't have to ask these guys to clean their plates!

PANDA PALS

For pandas living in the **Sichuan Giant Panda Sanctuaries** in the Qionglai and Jiajin Mountains of Sichuan Province, China, life is never lonely. Their home is the **largest giant panda habitat**. More than 30 percent of the world's panda population lives in this protected place filled with natural reserves and scenic parks—and there's definitely room for them. The habitat is 3,569 square miles.

ZOO STAR

There's a lot of love for **Colo** the gorilla. Born in 1956, Colo (short for Columbus, Ohio) was the first-ever gorilla born in captivity. After her mother rejected her, the Columbus Zoo raised her like a human baby. The zoo staff even dressed her in baby clothes! Little Colo thrived, and now she is the **oldest living gorilla in captivity**.

A special gorilla like Colo deserves a special birthday. When she turned 58 on December 22, 2014, she celebrated with the zoo staff, volunteers, and guests. No birthday cake for her though. She enjoyed her favorite treat: tomatoes!

WHEE!

With a name like **Truffles**, you might think this guinea pig stays close to the ground. But on April 6, 2012, he cleared a gap of 18.89 inches in Fife, Scotland, the **longest jump by a guinea pig**. He beat the former record of almost 12 inches twice now. But the previous record holder doesn't mind, because it was Truffles himself. Sounds like he's giving himself quite a workout!

BABYPALOOZA!

On February 28, 1974, the Miller family of Louisiana had quite a day. That was the day their hamster gave birth to 26 babies—the **largest hamster litter**! That's a whole lot of cuteness. The average litter size for a hamster is eight. And on August 17, 1992, Australian Ruth Winkler's guinea pig, **Casperina**, had the **largest guinea pig litter**. Nine guinea pig babies were born that day and they all survived.

ULTIMATE FACT:

Hamsters are nocturnal. They sleep during the day and wake up at night, running in wheels, digging, and crawling through tubes. So if you're a night owl, a hamster might just be the perfect pet!

LONG-LIVED RODENTS

Ever wonder how long caged gerbils, hamsters, and guinea pigs can live? Well, these three Guinness World Records holders share a unique talent for longevity.

Sahara, a Mongolian gerbil owned by Aaron Milsone of Michigan, is the **longest-lived caged gerbil**. This well-adjusted pet thrived until the age of 8 years, 4.5 months—more than twice the average lifespan of 3 to 4 years.

Compare that statistic to the **longest-lived caged guinea pig**, **Snowball**. Belonging to M. A. Wall of the UK, Snowball lived happily until the age of 14 years and 10.5 months. The average guinea pig lives 4 to 8 years!

If you're a hamster, chances are you won't have a long life; the average pet lives between 18 and 24 months. But Karen Smeaton's hamster defied the odds. He lived to be 4 and a half years old, making him the **oldest hamster ever**!

CHAPTER 5
Rabbits! Snakes! Scales!
And More . . .

These record holders come from all corners of the globe, slithering, scurrying, and even running—on water! You'll get the skinny on the world's heaviest snake, meet a reptile well into his teen years, and take a look at a frog with skin so translucent, you can see his heart!

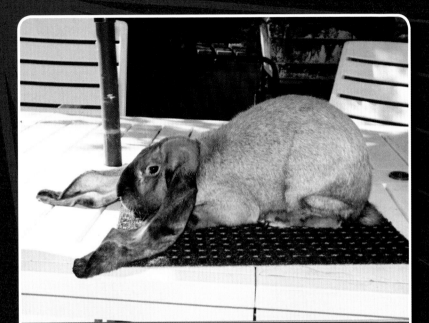

FUNNY BUNNY

It's not a surprise that **Nipper's Geronimo**, an English Lop, is a Guinness World Records holder with ears this long. The **longest-ever rabbit ears** measured 31.125 inches in a complete span at the American Rabbit Breeders Association National Show in Kansas. Nicknamed "Nipper's Guinness," he was a tortoiseshell buck born on May 10, 2003. He died in 2006.

CARROT CRUNCHER

No one has to tell **Darius**, a Flemish giant rabbit, to eat his vegetables. The world's **longest rabbit**, who measured a record-worthy 4 feet, 3 inches on April 6, 2010, eats over 4,000 carrots a year—that's more than 10 per day on average!

MULTIPLYING BUNNIES

They just kept coming . . . and coming . . . and coming. On May 17, 2008, during the Magic Congress in Saint-Vincent, Aosta, Italy, performers **Walter Rolfo** and **Piero Ustignani** pulled a total of 300 rabbits out of thin air! It's no trick they set the record for **most rabbits pulled out of a magician's hat**.

SLUGGIN' AROUND

The largest-known land gastropod is the African giant snail, and one named **Gee Geronimo** was the **largest snail** of all. Measuring 15.5 inches from snout to tail when fully extended, with a shell length of 10.75 inches, the gastropod was owned by Christopher Hudson of the UK and was collected in Sierra Leone in 1978.

ULTIMATE FACT:
The African giant snail might look like a regular garden snail, but its shell measures an average of 8 inches. All gastropods have a muscular foot for walking or swimming!

MAKING HISSSSSSTORY

Slithering her way into the record books is **Medusa**, the **longest snake in captivity ever**, owned by Full Moon Productions in Missouri. When she was measured on October 12, 2011, the reticulated python was 25 feet, 2 inches long.

ULTIMATE FACT:
Reticulated pythons are usually 10 to 20 feet long, making them the world's longest snake species.

DADDY LONG LEGS

Big Daddy, a Japanese spider crab that lives at SEA LIFE Blackpool aquarium in the UK, boasts some record-breaking limbs. The longest measures a whopping 4 feet, 8.5 inches, the **longest leg on a crab**.

HEAVY DUTY

The **heaviest crustacean on land** is the **robber crab**. It lives on tropical islands and atolls in the Indo-Pacific. How heavy is this crustacean? An average weight is 5 pounds, 8 ounces with a leg span of 39 inches—though some have grown up to 9 pounds. What does this big guy like to eat? Rotting coconuts!

VENOMOUS HEAVYWEIGHT

Not a fan of snakes? You'll want to avoid the **eastern diamondback rattlesnake** then. It's the world's **heaviest venomous snake** and is found in the southeastern United States. The heaviest on record weighed in at 34 pounds and was 7 feet, 9 inches long.

DRAGON KEEPER

Nik Vernon of the UK took such good care of **Guinness**, his bearded dragon, that he lived 16 years, 129 days, making him the **oldest bearded dragon ever**! Bearded dragons generally live to about 8 years in the wild in Australia and typically a maximum of 14 years in captivity. Why "bearded"? The label refers to the place under the reptile's throat that darkens when it's feeling anxious!

WATERY WONDER

Walking on water? No problem for the **Common basilisk lizard** of South America. Not only can it walk on water using all fours, it can run bipedally at a speed of 5 feet a second for almost 15 feet before sinking, making it the **largest water walker**.

LITTLE CROC

You might miss this little guy if you aren't looking carefully. The **smallest crocodilian** in the world is the **dwarf caiman** of northern South America. Females rarely exceed a length of 4 feet, and males top out at 4 feet, 11 inches.

A TRUE GIANT

The Galápagos tortoise is the largest living species of tortoise. And the **largest tortoise** on record is **Goliath**, who lived at the Life Fellowship Bird Sanctuary in Seffner, Florida, from 1960 to 2002. Goliath lived up to his name—he was 4 feet, 5 inches long; 3 feet, 4 inches wide; and 2 feet, 3 inches high. And he must have eaten a lot of leaves: Goliath weighed 920 pounds.

A LONG LIFE

The Grand Cayman blue iguana is the **longest-lived lizard species**, and one lizard can claim the crown for outliving them all. **Godzilla**, an adult male, was captured alive in 1950 by naturalist Ira Thompson. He thought Godzilla was about 15 years old. In 1985, Ira sold Godzilla to an animal dealer in the US, who kept him for five years and then donated him to the Gladys Porter Zoo in Texas. He lived there until his death in 2004, which means he spent 54 years in captivity and had an estimated total lifespan of 69 years.

HEART OF GLASS

You can see right inside these lime-green-hued frogs, the **most-transparent amphibians** in the world. Native to the Central and South American rain forests, the frogs, formally of the family **Centrolenidae**, have partially transparent abdominal skin that resembles frosted glass, earning them the nickname glass frogs. Their hearts, livers, and guts can be easily seen when looking at the frog from underneath.

Best Served Chilled

NO CAFFEINE
SODIUM FREE
NOTHING ARTIFICIAL

365

Lem
Lim

Our friends in the sky and water come together swimmingly when it comes to being incredible. The sky's the limit—literally—with what these creatures have achieved. From a parrot with serious basketball skills to a fish that can swim under a limbo bar, it's time to soar into more records!

CHIRPING CHATTERBOX

Once this bird starts talking, he might not be able to stop. That's because **Oskar** is able to say 148 words, making him the bird with the **largest vocabulary**. Oskar is a budgie owned by Gabriela Danisch of Germany. *Talk* about expressing himself!

FEATHERED FRIEND

With their pretty colors and sociable personalities, cockatiels are one of the most popular pet birds in the USA. Native to Australia, the average cockatiel lives 15 to 25 years, but clearly no one has told that to **Sammy**. As of February 3, 2015, he had aged 30 years, 186 days. Bought for her by a college roommate in 1984, Diane Miksch from St. Pete Beach, Florida, is the proud owner of the **oldest living cockatiel**.

NOTHIN' BUT NET

This hoops star schools the competition! **Zac**, a harlequin macaw, holds the Guinness World Records title for **most slam dunks by a parrot**, getting 22 in just one minute. His owners, Julie and Ed Cardoza, are parrot trainers, and Zac is one of many birds in a traveling parrot show that performs at parties, libraries, and schools. Besides being an ace baller, Zac can bike, scooter, skateboard, roll over, and raise a flag, and he has a vocabulary of 100 words. After all this, Zac might be thirsty. Good thing he also holds the record for the **most soda cans opened by a parrot**! He made short work of 35 ring-pulls in one minute using just his beak.

LOOK WHO'S TALKING

The bird with the **largest vocabulary ever** was another budgie, **Puck**, owned by Camille Jordan of California. Puck had a whopping 1,728 words at his disposal before passing away in 1994.

OLD-AGE PARROT

Aged at least 80 years, 107 days as of September 15, 2014, **Cookie** has outlived most of his kind. According to a Brookfield Zoo ledger, the **oldest living parrot** arrived at the zoo in May 1934 and was estimated to be at least one year old. The zoo gave him a "hatch date" of June 30, 1933.

SOMETHING FISHY

Albert Einstein, a calico fantail goldfish, isn't content with just swimming around the fishbowl. He likes to perform! He's the **fish with the largest repertoire of tricks**. He can eat from a person's hand, swim through a hoop, swim through a tunnel that's twice the length of his body, swim under a limbo bar, play soccer by pushing a tiny soccer ball across the floor of his tank and into a goal, and play fetch! Albert Einstein was trained by his owner, Dean Pomerleau, at the Fish School in Pennsylvania.

A LIFESAVING PARROT

Pets give us love and affection, and their loyalty can know no bounds. That was the case with a grey parrot named **Charlie**. In December 1999, Christmas lights igniting curtains caused a fire in Patricia Tunnicliffe's home in the UK. Thankfully Charlie's squawks, which turned to shouts as the flames began to spread, woke up Patricia. Because of him, she managed to get her five children out of the smoke-filled house unharmed. Charlie is the Guinness World Records holder for **most lives saved by a parrot**, but sadly, he did not survive the fire. The brave pet belonged to a friend of the family, and it was too dangerous for Patricia to go back into the house to rescue him.

ULTIMATE FACT: Called the "Einsteins of the parrot world," African Greys can match the intellectual level of a five-year-old child. They're talkative, too, and can mimic up to 2,000 sounds.

FROM GOLD TO SILVER

Little did seven-year-old Peter Hand from the UK know that when he won a fish at a roll-a-penny fairground stall in 1956, his fish—that he named **Tish**—would go on to become the **oldest goldfish ever**. Tish lived in a glass bowl on a hallway table, and his scales turned to silver as he grew older. When Tish died in 1999, aged at least 43 years, the Hands buried him in a shady corner of their yard, honoring Tish's dislike of direct sunlight.

A GIANT GOLDFISH

Joris Gijsbers's goldfish wouldn't fit into a regular goldfish bowl. That's because Joris was the proud owner of the world's **longest goldfish ever**. This vibrant orange-finned wonder measured 18.7 inches from snout to tail fin on March 24, 2003, in the Netherlands. Nothing fishy about that!

CHAPTER 7
We Love Animals

Whether they're big or small, hairy or finned, caged or in a pasture, animals make the world a special place. Playing with them, snuggling with them, or simply watching them can make us happier—not to mention the physical benefits of riding a horse or taking a dog for a walk. So we'll wrap up this book about our record-setting friends with a doggie "I do," some big treats, and a group of people who came together for a cause we can all support!

What a difference a day can make. Specifically September 28, 2012—the day that 100 employees of **Mars Petcare** in the UK worked together to sort 9,253 pounds, 14 ounces of cat food for charity. It was the **most pet food donated to charity in 24 hours**, and the entire process, from weighing the pet food to the final delivery, took fewer than five hours.

DO YOU HAVE THAT IN LARGE?

You'd need a giant refrigerator to store this jumbo-sized pet food package. Measuring 9 feet, 10 inches by 5 feet, 10 inches by 1 foot, 7 inches, the **largest pet food container** was displayed on October 28, 2013, in São Paulo, Brazil, at a conference for members of the pet food industry.

DOGGIE DRESS-UP!

The **Beggin' Pet Parade** in St. Louis, Missouri, was home to some of the wackiest, cutest, and furriest costumes ever on parade. February 12, 2012, marks the day they achieved the  **most dogs in costumed attire**. A grand total of 1,326 hounds put on their costumes and showed off their finery for the crowd.

BIG BISCUIT

The **largest dog biscuit** weighed 617 pounds! It was baked to celebrate the tenth anniversary of **Hampshire Pet Products**, and once the record was achieved, it was broken into small pieces and given to dogs at the Humane Society in Joplin, Missouri.

Love was in the air on May 19, 2007. On that spring day, the **largest dog "wedding" ceremony** was held at the **Bow Wow Vows** event in Littleton, Colorado. One hundred seventy-eight dog pairs sealed their "marriages" with a bark. Even though the ceremony wasn't legally binding, the doggie brides and grooms all received complimentary wedding certificates to remember their special day. Their courtships were on the short side: all the dog couples met during a speed-dating session right before the ceremony!